SMALL TOWNS, BLACK LIVES

This book is a gift
from
The Noyes Museum of Art

SMALL TOWNS, BLACK LIVES

African American Communities in Southern New Jersey

Wendel A. White

Introduction by Charles Ashley Stainback

Essays by Deborah Willis, Stedman Graham, and Clement Alexander Price

The Noyes Museum of Art
Oceanville, New Jersey

This catalogue is published on the occasion of the exhibition *Small Towns, Black Lives: African American Communities in Southern New Jersey,* organized by the Noyes Museum of Art.

Exhibition Itinerary

The Noyes Museum of Art
Oceanville, New Jersey
January 18 to April 27, 2003

Johnson and Johnson
New Brunswick, New Jersey
May 15 to July 15, 2003

The exhibition was organized by the Noyes Museum of Art with the support of the New Jersey State Council on the Arts, Department of State; the New Jersey Council for the Humanities, a state partner of the National Endowment for the Humanities; New Jersey Historical Commission, Department of State; the Geraldine R. Dodge Foundation; Johnson and Johnson; Bally's Park Place Entertainment; the Mr. and Mrs. Fred W. Noyes Foundation; the Odessa F. and Henry D. Kahrs Charitable Trust, David L. Wallen, Raymond F. Maguire, and First Union Bank Trustees, with additional support from the Richard Stockton College of New Jersey.

First Edition 2003

Edited by Mary Christian and Carla Williams
Designed by Tsang Seymour Design, New York

The text of this book is composed in Adobe Trade Gothic
Color separations by Professional Graphics, Inc., Rockford, Illinois
Printed and bound by CS Graphics PTE Ltd., Singapore

©2003 by the Noyes Museum of Art. All rights reserved.

No part of this publication may be reproduced in any form by any electronic or mechanical means (including photocopying, recording, or information storage and retrieval) without permission in writing from the Noyes Museum of Art.

Works by Wendel A. White ©Wendel A. White

Library of Congress Cataloging-in-Publication Data

White, Wendel A., 1956-
  Small towns, Black lives : African American communities in southern New Jersey / Wendel A. White : introduction by Charles Ashley Stainback: essays by Deborah Willis, Stedman Graham, and Clement Alexander Price.— 1st ed.
    p. cm.
  Includes bibliographical references.
  ISBN 0-9723951-0-5
1. Photography, Artistic—Exhibitions. 2. African Americans—New Jersey—Portraits—Exhibitions. 3. African Americans—New Jersey—Social life and customs—20th century—Pictorial works—Exhibitions. 4. Cities and towns—New Jersey—Pictorial works—Exhibitions. 5. White, Wendel A., 1956—Exhibitions. I. Willis, Deborah, 1948- II. Graham, Stedman. III. Price, Clement Alexander, 1945- IV. Noyes Museum of Art. V. Title.
  TR647 .W47 2003
  779'.9974998'00496073—dc21
                                           2002014136

The Noyes Museum of Art
Lily Lake Road
Oceanville, New Jersey 08231
609.652.8848
www.noyesmuseum.org

CONTENTS

4   **FOREWORD**   Lawrence Schmidt

6   **PREFACE**   Wendel A. White

8   **INTRODUCTION**   Charles Ashley Stainback

10   **VISUAL TESTIMONY: THE PHOTOGRAPHS OF WENDEL A. WHITE**   Deborah Willis

14   **PORT REPUBLIC AND MORRIS BEACH**

40   **WHITESBORO AND CAPE MAY'S FRANKLIN STREET SCHOOL**

68   **WHITESBORO: A HOMETOWN REMEMBERED**   Stedman Graham

78   **GOULDTOWN AND SPRINGTOWN**

92   **SMALL GLOUCESTER, SWEDESBORO AND ELSMERE**

114   **LAWNSIDE AND CHESILHURST**

152   **ADAT BEYT MOSHEH AND NEWTONVILLE**

168   **HOME AND HEARTH: THE BLACK TOWN AND SETTLEMENT MOVEMENT OF SOUTHERN NEW JERSEY**
Clement Alexander Price

176   CHECKLIST OF THE EXHIBITION

178   FURTHER READING

179   ARTIST BIOGRAPHY

180   ACKNOWLEDGEMENTS

FOREWORD

Lawrence Schmidt
Executive Director, The Noyes Museum of Art

The Noyes Museum of Art, founded in 1983 as the vision of two incredible people of local legend, Fred and Ethel Noyes, has over the years grown and matured as a cultural institution. The only art museum in the southern region of the nation's most densely populated state, the Noyes strives to serve residents and visitors alike by collecting and exhibiting quality works that reflect the area's artistic vibrancy and heritage.

As the Noyes Museum of Art marks its twentieth anniversary, it is appropriate that it should focus the public's attention on art of exceptional quality and powerful voice, an artist of merit, themes of cultural and social relevance, and the region it serves. With Wendel A. White's work in *Small Towns, Black Lives: African American Communities in Southern New Jersey*, the Noyes Museum has found a perfect conjunction of these ideal focal qualities.

White's journey for *Small Towns* began in 1986, shortly after he relocated to the area to take a teaching position at Richard Stockton College. From his first visit to Cape May County's Whitesboro, a community founded by black entrepreneurs in the post-Reconstruction era, White realized there was more to the story. Indeed, what has evolved is the visual product of an artist's passion for his subject, but he has also added many other ingredients—including interviews, history, and a sense of place. While the story White has unfolded is unique, one finds themes that transcend a specific locale and speak to the experience not only of a people, but of a nation.

Projects like *Small Towns* do not simply happen; they spring from thought and enthusiasm into reality through dedicated effort and diligence. We are most appreciative of the many people who have contributed to the exhibition and its accompanying components. Foremost, we wish to acknowledge the artist, Wendel A. White, who has been a wonderful and eloquent partner for this endeavor. His keen insights and good humor propelled this project forward in an enjoyable and productive manner. Charles Stainback, guest curator, brought a wealth of knowledge and talent to the exhibition. Respected historian and long-time friend Clement Alexander Price, professor of history at Rutgers University, made important contributions to the project, including his good counsel, knowledge, and his essay in this catalogue. We are grateful to scholar Deborah Willis for inspiring Wendel A. White to start his odyssey with a visit to Whitesboro and for her catalogue essay placing White's work in the context of a rich tradition of photographs by black artists. We are indebted to Whitesboro's favorite son, Stedman Graham, for his support and contributions. Graham, by his accomplishments, exemplifies a proud spirit of determination in personal excellence, yet reminds us of our interconnectedness and the need to see the individual within the scope of community.

We are also grateful for the support of Johnson & Johnson; the New Jersey Council for the Humanities, a state partner of the National Endowment for the Humanities; Bally's Park Place Entertainment; the New Jersey State Council on the Arts, Department of State; The Geraldine R. Dodge Foundation; New Jersey Historical Commission, Department of State; the Mr. and Mrs. Fred W. Noyes Foundation; and the Odessa F. and Henry D. Kahrs Charitable Trust. We appreciate the collegial support of Richard Stockton College of New Jersey and its efforts in this project. We acknowledge Mary Christian and Carla Williams for their editing of the catalogue manuscripts; Patrick Seymour and Kei Matsuoka of Tsang Seymour Design for their outstanding vision with the design of the catalogue; the expertise and cooperation of Donna Ostrazewski and her staff at the Exhibition Alliance; and Hsiao-Ning Tu, who, as the museum's former curator of exhibitions and collections, first envisioned *Small Towns* as a project of the Noyes Museum. And, of course, the project could not have occurred without the contributions of the museum's staff and volunteers including Gay Walling, Corrine Sheeran, Ann Van Hise, Saul Cosme, and Shirley Kanas.

Through the organization and presentation of this exhibition, the Noyes Museum continues to fulfill the vision of its founders: to become a leading arts resource in the region. As we enter into our third decade, it gives us great pleasure to present Wendel A. White and his unique perspective on this aspect of life in southern New Jersey.

PREFACE

Wendel A. White

I began making photographs for this project in 1989 after a casual remark from Deborah Willis in which she told me about a community called Whitesboro that she had visited as a child. In the summer of 1989 I drove to Whitesboro, walked around, and made a few photographs. My first conversation was with Rev. George Thompson of the First Baptist Church. Our discussion led to contacts throughout Whitesboro and I began making portraits inside homes and businesses. Many of the longtime residents are descendants of families that moved to Whitesboro to escape the race riots, unemployment, and oppression of late-nineteenth-century North Carolina.

    The project started without a thesis, simply a willingness to invest time and energy on pictures and the fellowship of time spent in black communities. Throughout the summer of 1989, as I photographed various people and events, it was clear that the stories and oral histories I encountered were essential to the social landscape. In the past thirteen years I have struggled to adequately define a form for the images and the narrative, however I find myself compelled to continue in spite of my awkwardness. The process established in Whitesboro has remained with me for more than a decade. I often make contact through churches or individuals and I am drawn to the informal and ordinary views of small-town life.

The photographs of the Port Republic cemetery began as the result of another casual comment, this time from Joseph Stevenson. All but one of the graves identify veterans of the U.S. Colored Troops, and they are located on a road without any other sign of a black settlement. These pictures led to my first specific use of genealogical research techniques, text in combination with the photographs, and other archival materials as subjects of my photography. Researching the Port Republic site rejuvenated my enthusiasm for the remarkable history of black communities. Reconstructing the story of this black settlement, whose only physical representation consists of five headstones, changed my work to include remnants of rural black settlements. The result has become a project that includes portraits, landscapes, architecture, artifacts, archival documents, and narrative text that uses historical material, but is not offered as a history.

My mother's family narrative is closely tied to the purchase of a farm in rural North Carolina by my great-grandfather after the Civil War. Before my mother died we spoke several times about whether she would like to be buried on the farm and she was unable to decide between rural traditions of the family and urban/suburban reality of her life. I chose to bury her near her brothers, parents, and grandparents on the farm in North Carolina, because some of her best stories were childhood memories of summers on the farm. The photographs in *Small Towns, Black Lives* are made in communities that have no direct connection to my personal history, but they are representations of a connection and context.

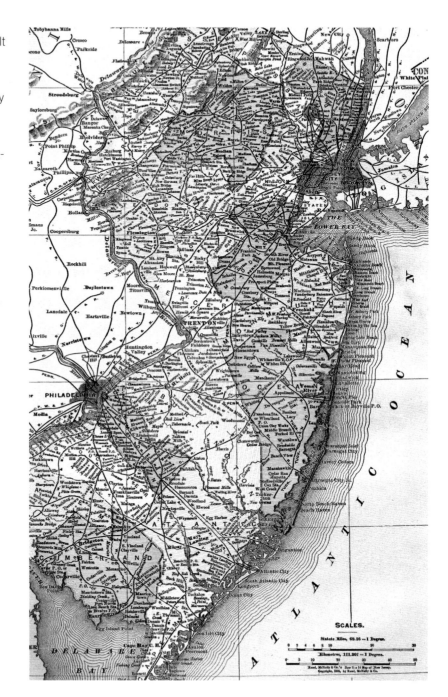

Rand, McNally & Co.'s New 11 x 14 Map of New Jersey 1895

INTRODUCTION

Charles Ashley Stainback

A single photographic print may be "news," a "portrait," "art," or, "documentary," or any of these, all of them, or none. Among the tools of social science graphs, statistics, maps, and text, documentation by photograph now is assuming place.

Dorothea Lange, 1940

We all have seen them and most of us have them—those thick picture albums of our family history. The family trees of proud, familiar-looking strangers lined up from oldest to youngest, or relatives standing straight and stiff next to a house we vaguely recognize. These not-so-candid snapshots are as captivating and reassuring as they are universal and odd. As images, they give us essential clues to the long-lost stories of an unwritten family history. In looking back, they summon the future.

As the renowned documentary photographer Dorothea Lange acutely observed in photography's centennial year, even the casual snapshot can take on multiple meanings or uses. And somewhere among the casual vernacular documents in the family album and the news, portrait, art, or documentary photographs are pictures that are difficult to classify because they blend those borders. When Lange wrote about documentary photography in 1940, the term was relatively new. An outgrowth of documentary films of the 1930s in Great Britain and developed through the heyday of America's influential picture magazines *Life* and *Look*, the documentary photograph quickly became an important tool for social awareness and change. And today, from illustrated news magazines to twenty-four-hour television news coverage, the photograph has displaced the printed word as the way we receive much of our daily information. For photography's first hundred years, most photographs were seen only as tools for recording the field of vision before the camera's lens, but as Lange observed, not all photographs are records, artifacts, or documents of indisputable veracity. Her assertion that a single photograph could assume an array of roles and functions was prophetic of issues in the medium that we encounter today, when many photographs are no longer the objective record of what was before the lens, but are manipulated by computer.

Photography has not only changed the way we understood history and the way we see it, but also how we read about it: just the mention of Kent State, the moon landing, Iwo Jima, and the World Trade Center brings images to mind that we all saw in the newspaper or on TV, even though only a relatively small percentage of people actually witnessed those events in person. In a little over 160 years the photographic image has transformed not only how we understand history, it has fundamentally altered how we view ourselves. If the victor writes history, then who commits it to memory? The photographer records the collective memory of our culture.

The photographs in Wendel White's *Small Towns, Black Lives* are the kinds of hybrids Lange described and anticipated in her statement. The exhibition and book form a personal album revealing the layers of meaning and history that he carefully uncovered. His project to document African American communities in southern New Jersey began in much the same way that many photographers before him had set out to record a place or people. Having grown up in urban and suburban communities, he realized that there was much he didn't know about the heritage of small town African American communities that were right in his own backyard, about people he vaguely recognized in the family album and those whom he had never seen before, but who traveled the same roads and shared a similar past and hopes for the future.

White's project began with making pictures in Whitesboro, New Jersey, a town founded by African Americans and named after George H. White (no relation), a congressman from North Carolina. As the great-grandson of a slave, the photographer's idea to document the people of New Jersey towns like Whitesboro was at first small and sincere, but it then grew into a passion that would become a thirteen-year-long project. Over that time he spoke with countless people, made thousands of photographs, and came to better understand the context of his own family's rich heritage and history as it intersected with the much larger, overlooked story and struggle of African Americans. Settlements and residents of towns like Whitesboro have been trivialized by surrounding communities for generations, but their contributions are poignantly expressed in images such as that of the graves of the Civil War soldiers of the U.S. Colored Troops that lie in an unmarked cemetery in Port Republic. These men served their country, but no plaque or historic roadside marker was near to guide the curious.

Neither stridently documentary nor self-consciously arty, White's images straddle two worlds. They adopt the cool reserve of certain recent fine art photographers—Lewis Baltz, for example. Yet he is also true to the sincere lens of many of photography's great documentarians—such as Lange, or Jacob Riis, who documented the horrid slum condition in New York's Lower East Side, or Lewis Hine, who took part in the influential Farm Security Administration documentary project from 1937 to 1942. White has produced a body of work that is uniquely personal and profoundly informative. His photographs thoughtfully ask us to look without preconceptions at the history he has uncovered.

White's work reads as an expanded family album—personal, poignant, and loving. These captions provide an intellectual connection— explanatory text fills in the salient facts of who, what, where, when, and how— for the otherwise emotional response that we might have to each image. The exhibition and catalogue *Small Towns, Black Lives* is part of a much larger personal and educational journey for White. His process began with inquiring, listening, and researching; then he made the individual photographs. These carefully researched and wrought photographs are images for which a patient, careful viewing brings great rewards.

And as a culture we have become increasingly accustomed to seeing the world and understanding our place in it through photographs. White's images preserve forgotten histories. Like many news, portrait, art, documentary, and even amateur photographers before him, White makes images that help us with the task of remembering—and more importantly, with the responsibility of not forgetting.

VISUAL TESTIMONY:
THE PHOTOGRAPHS OF WENDEL A. WHITE

Deborah Willis

As modern visual poets, [black photographers] were ... concerned with locating and reproducing the beauty and fragility of the race, the ironic humor of everyday life, the dream life of a people.

Robin D.G. Kelley

American photography began as an art woven from commonplace prosperity and created an inventory of everyday experience.

Merry A. Foresta

Wendel A. White strives to capture the "dream life of a people" through his photographs that offer an alternative reading and analysis of history. Combining formal portraiture with text, White creates a visually engaging experience between subject and photographer and collective memory and cultural practices. The "commonplace prosperity" found in his works provides a view of America that incorporates the preservation of life and the survival of a culture. Looking at his photographs of black towns in New Jersey, I can vividly imagine how these towns served their constituents at the moment of their founding.

The photographs sparked my interest not just because of their historical value, but also because of my personal memories. When I was a young girl, my parents often drove from Philadelphia to Lawnside, New Jersey, on Sunday afternoons after church services. On Saturday and Sunday, at least once a month in the winter and two or three times a month in the summer, we would pile into the car to visit relatives and eat corn on the cob and barbecue cooked on open pits. I knew then that Lawnside was a special place, segregated by choice, with everyone enjoying their day off, telling stories, playing cards or checkers, jumping rope, and sharing in their community pride. We also often visited relatives in Whitesboro and Chesilhurst in southern New Jersey. Our family and friends had second homes in those areas and were comforted by their isolation and sense of communal living. White's photographs speak to the endurance and resilience of these black towns and their inhabitants.

The history of black towns is grounded in community pride and self-governance. More than fifty black towns were established in the United States, many in southern New Jersey including Lawnside, Gouldtown, Springtown, and Whitesboro. They provided opportunities for economic advancement and social uplift, and they were often seen by their residents as protective havens. Many of these towns were and are unknown to the larger society, but others have achieved some distinction. They include Boley, Oklahoma; Institute, West Virginia; Mound Bayou, Mississippi; Grambling, Louisiana; Nicodemus, Kansas; and Allensworth, California. Each town had a unique beginning. For example, Allen Allensworth, who was born a slave, founded the first all-black town in California. Lawnside, New Jersey, became the first African American incorporated municipality in 1926. Originally known as Snowhill, it had been established in the latter part of the eighteenth century and became a stop on the Underground Railroad. Gouldtown was named after a black man, Benjamin Gould, who married Elizabeth Fenwick, granddaughter of the English nobleman John Fenwick, a wealthy colonist.

The photographs of these towns are a reconnection with the past, a remembering of community, individuals, and a legacy bound in pride and pain. Using a contemporary voice, White revisits the towns, some of which are more than two hundred years old, photographing the descendants of some of the original townspeople and contextualizing their experiences with words. He explores the connections between slavery and its impact on free blacks, miscegenation, the Underground Railroad, the abolitionist movement, black family life, community history, entrepreneurship, and patriotism.

White began this project in the mid-1980s. Like most photographers of this period, he was interested in documenting Americana in the model of the Farm Security Administration photographers. After moving to southern New Jersey to teach photography, he began taking pictures of his newfound community. Reflecting his interest in the land, White made a series of photographs of the rural and urban New Jersey landscape. His photographs during this period visually analyzed the relationship between the public and private history of black Americans in New Jersey. By focusing on the land, White uncovered a lost history of the people in communities in southern New Jersey. He writes, "Photography is a way for me to satisfy my curiosity about how things work physically and philosophically."

From its beginning, this project was a self-conscious endeavor. As White explains: "The project is a personal record of my interest in historically African American communities in southern counties of New Jersey … This work is not presented as a historical resource but as an artist's journal of travel and discovery." White looked inside and outside each community, linking enslaved and free blacks of the nineteenth century to working and middle-class blacks in the twenty-first century. What is fascinating and engaging about the photographs is the depiction of domestic, military, political, and economic life through a combination of portraiture, landscape, and the written word. White's photographs form an historical narrative that transcends memory and is informed by his juxtaposition of text and image. "My work uses historical and documentary text combined with images that seek to describe the experience in black communities with this region," he writes, "the stories of these communities in the southern part of the state are remarkable and generally under-represented in literature and documentary images."

The visual curiosity that White describes is represented in his first project—photographs of the burial sites of black soldiers who fought in the Civil War. White memorializes the forgotten soldiers by photographing the weatherworn headstones and digitally juxtaposing biographical text about the black men who served in the war. The photographs symbolize the experiences of the black soldiers who believed in and fought for freedom for black people. They are quiet reminders of the past and, with the current debate on reparations, remind us of the promise of the Civil War and Reconstruction. This subject continued to absorb White as he researched and photographed the desolate sites and collected the related archival records.

White later broadened the project and began photographing descendants of the Civil War soldiers and other families in the area. He also incorporated text into these formal portraits, often placing the photographic images on the left side of the frame and the words on the right. The result is a book-like format that resembles both a nineteenth-century travel album and a personal family album. White serves not only as the image-maker but also the biographer, narrator, and participant. The landscape in which he locates and revives the community's history is transformed into a portable photographic exhibition, growing each time the photographs are displayed.

These symbolic photographs, imbued with communal pride, respect, and mystery, provoke emotion in the viewer. They encourage us to think about the history of places like Gouldtown and about how the townspeople maintained their close-knit communities. White offers us clues in the photograph *Trinity A. M. E. Church, Gouldtown, N.J. 1993*, which depicts a community room with a banner draped over the top indicating the 200th anniversary of the church founded in 1792. Biblical scriptures are written on a chalkboard with the words "Persistant [*sic*] and "Prayer" underlined. The image is a simple one—American flag, crucifix, podium, desk and tables—devoid of people, but we feel their presence and their sense of spirituality and community. Lesson plans, photographs, bible verses, and hymnals tell us about Gouldtown's inheritance of endurance.

Photographs of such women as Mrs. Tecolia Salters of Chesilhurst, Mrs. Sarah Lucile Stewart-Mitchell of Swedesboro, Dr. Merrie Hill, and Mrs. Elaine Edwards symbolize inherited family and community pride. White contextualizes their individual histories by giving us signifiers within the image and the text. For example, Dr. Hill is seated in her living room; her demeanor is regal as she looks directly into the camera. Her Persian rug, vinyl-covered furniture, mirror, antique table, and silk curtains reveal her status as a middle-class resident of the community. The photographs on the end table memorialize weddings and other family gatherings, but the text tells us her history and that her uncle, Alvin Williams, originally owned the property.

In contrast, the striking portrait of Mrs. Salters is of a woman who has worked the land. This widow is comfortable with the camera and directs her gaze past the photographer to the viewer. She smiles with her eyes as she stretches one arm across the back of the sofa, feeling its texture, and places

her other arm next to her body. We see touches of her handicraft in the crocheted doilies and throw pillows on the sofa. Her walls are decorated with small genre scenes. The text enhances the iconography of the portrait by explaining that Mrs. Salters farmed the land that she owned and sold her produce in Philadelphia on the weekends. The photograph of Mrs. Edwards and Mrs. Stewart-Mitchell is a symbol of community pride and resistance against Jim Crow laws. The Lodge, its paneled walls filled with photographs and text panels, was once a segregated school and the building is now registered as an historic site.

White's work interprets the history of black towns and explains how personal strife influenced their survival. His photographs, which portray people as they wish to be seen, are both affirming and challenging. Images of family homes that include views of people's private photographs affirm the subjects' place in history and memory. The text challenges the standard historical record and provides us with access to a world that might easily have been forgotten. The stories White constructs through words and photographs give us a complex history full of charm, irony, pride, and personal revelations.

Tiffany's Beans, Greens and Birds
Whitesboro, New Jersey

Newtonville
Weymouth
Forest Grove
Minotola
Hebron
Landisville
Pancoast
Richland
Mizpah
Harbor
Wheat Rosa
Maine Ave
Buena
Vineland
S. Vineland
Clayville
Millville
Milmay
Manumuskin Creek
Manumuskin
Port Elizabeth
Tuckahoe
Estelville P. O.
or Estelle Sta.
English Creek
Buck Hill
A T
A N D

Port Republic and Morris Beach
Atlantic County

Moss Mill Road
Port Republic, New Jersey, 1990

The residents of the Moss Mill road community had various occupations including farmer, "coalyer," millworker, and odd-jobman in the town. Between 1863 and 1865 Josiah Boling, Charles Boling, William Lee, Eli Boling, James Trusty, Alexander Smith, and Moses Miller served in the 24th and 25th Regiments of the U.S. Colored Troops during the Civil War. The community they established existed from 1850 until at least 1916. There were probably twenty to twenty-five residents at various times, and as many as fifteen were buried in the cemetery on Moss Mill road. The only headstones that remain mark the graves of Charles Boling, Josiah Boling, Samuel Boling, William Lee, and Alexander Smith.

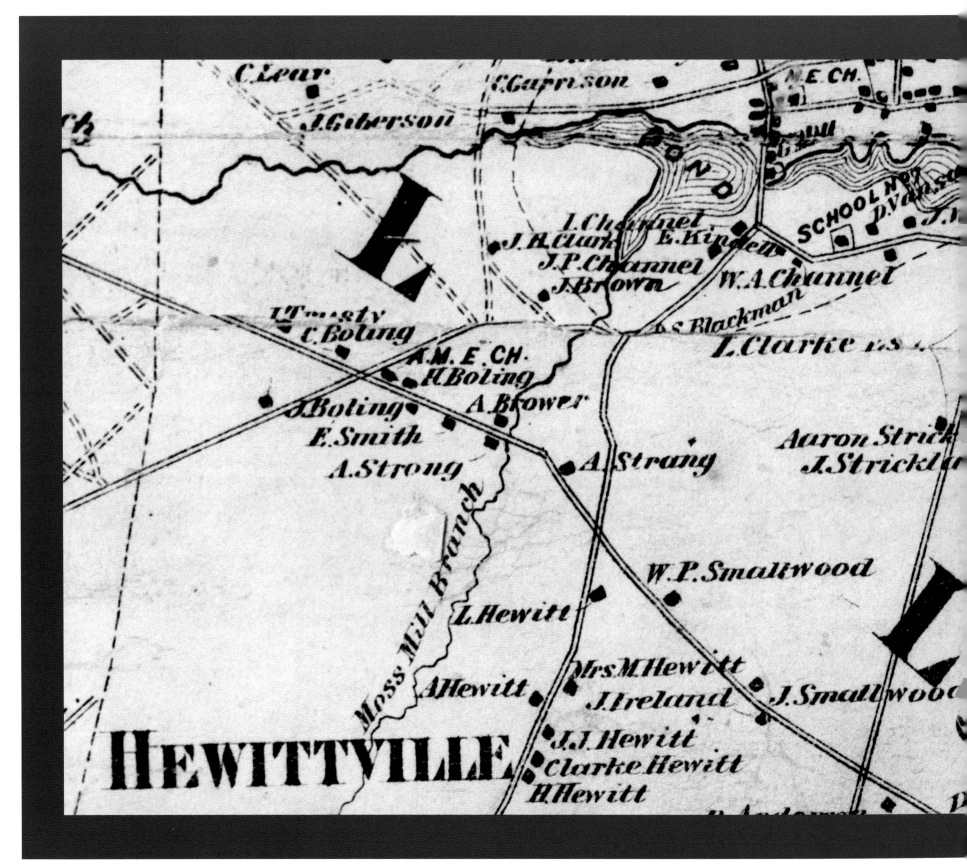

Beers, Comstock and Cline Map
Port Republic and Galloway Township
New Jersey, 1872

In 1849 Henry and Grace Boling and their children Josiah, Deborah, Sarah, Charles, Rebecca, Beulah, Eli, and Mary moved to Port Republic from Woodbury, New Jersey. Henry Boling purchased a little over two acres from "Lewis Clark and wife" for the sum of $32.25 on February 11, 1857. This formed the first purchase of land in what eventually became a small African American community. In 1872, when this map was drawn, the community included six homes and an African Methodist Episcopal church.

Alexander Smith Grave
Port Republic, New Jersey, 1990

Alexander Smith was born October 9, 1833 in Weymouth, New Jersey. His father, Samuel Smith Sr. was born in 1784. He had at least two brothers, Isaac Smith and Samuel Smith, Jr. In 1859 Alexander married Deborah Boling, daughter of Henry and Grace Boling. Smith served during the Civil War in Company B, 25th Regiment of the U.S. Colored Troops. In 1872 the couple moved to Atlantic City, where their sons James and John were born. In 1909, at age seventy-five, he returned to Port Republic; he died February 23, 1910.

Charles Boling Grave
Port Republic, New Jersey, 1990

Charles Boling was born February 26, 1840, in Woodbury, New Jersey. In 1867 he married Ann Eliza Trusty, daughter of Alexander and Isabel Trusty. Between 1869 and 1876 they had five children—Walter, Henry, Samuel, Charlott, and William—none of whom survived their parents. Charles Boling served during the Civil War in Company B, 25th Regiment of the U.S. Colored Troops and died March 5, 1916, in Port Republic.

Josiah Boling Grave
Port Republic, New Jersey, 1990

Josiah Boling was born in 1834 Woodbury, New Jersey, and died May 27, 1909 in Atlantic City. At the age of sixty-three on December 30, 1897, he married forty-eight-year-old Rose Zella Smith (Alexander Smith's niece). The first marriage for each of them; they did not have any children. Rose Zella Boling died in Atlantic City February 23, 1924, "apparently frozen to death." Josiah Boling served during the Civil War in Company B, 25th Regiment of the U.S. Colored Troops and is buried in the cemetery on land once owned by his parents.

Samuel S. Boling Grave
Port Republic, New Jersey, 1990

Samuel Boling was born on June 26, 1872, the third child of Charles and Ann Eliza Boling. He married a woman named "Carey," but there is no record of her last name, when they married, or whether they had children; Carey P. Boling was named executor of her father-in-law's will and lived in Port Republic at the time of his death. Samuel Boling died May 9, 1915.

William Lee Grave
Port Republic, New Jersey, 1990

Although William Lee is buried in the Moss Mill Road cemetery, it is not clear whether he ever lived in the Port Republic community. He did serve with Eli Boling during the Civil War in Company I, 24th Regiment of the U.S. Colored Troops. At the time of his death James Trusty, Eli Boling, and Charles Boling filed claims against his estate for a total of $30.30. The value of William Lee's estate was $578, which included the proceeds from the sale of sixteen acres in Egg Harbor City, New Jersey.

Boling Children at School
Port Republic, New Jersey, 1911

The photographs are from the collection of Doris Mollick, Port Republic, New Jersey. The girl in the lower image is identified as "Annie Boling," standing with her class at the Port Republic School. The boy in the upper image is identified as "Johnnie Boling," also with his class outside the Port Republic School.

View of Morris Beach from Jobs Point Road
Morris Beach, New Jersey, 2000

Jennie Morris was a mortician from Philadelphia in 1939 when she purchased the property from Elijah R. Morehouse for fifteen thousand dollars—creating the Morris Beach community in Egg Harbor Township, New Jersey. The property was subdivided and houses were sold as summer homes to African Americans living in Philadelphia and New Jersey.

Bethune Avenue
Morris Beach, New Jersey, 2000

Inside the Morris Beach community, looking toward the single access road to enter and exit the settlement. Although once an exclusively African American summer resort community, there are increasingly diverse year-round residents as the original owners and their children have gradually less connection to Morris Beach and sell the homes in an open real estate market.

Former Community Center
Morris Beach, New Jersey, 2000

Now used as a private home, this structure served as a common building or community center during the earlier years of the settlement. In addition, residents used the space for Sunday worship services that were usually non-denominational, due to the diverse religious affiliations of the community.

Jack Trower's House
Morris Beach, New Jersey, 2000

Jack Trower was the original owner of this house, located next to the Jennie Morris house, facing the bay. Mr. Trower owned a catering business in Philadelphia. He was well known for a large mahogany speed boat.

Island Point S. Seaville P.O.
or Seaville Sta.
Goshen
Cape May C. H.
Dias Creek
Green Creek
Anglesea
Fishing Creek
Rio Grande
Bennett
Cold Spring Mid. Pine Holly
75 Sewells Pt.
Cape May Pt. Cape May 5

Whitesboro and Cape May's Franklin Street School
Cape May County

Whitesboro, New Jersey, 1990

From a 1930s real estate brochure:
"The climate is all that could be desired. You can get the ocean breezes constantly which is balmy and permeated with the ozone of the pines of Southern New Jersey. With your lungs full of this pure air you take on new life and vitality."

Audrey Lackey Real Estate Office
Whitesboro, New Jersey, 1989

Audrey Lackey moved to Whitesboro in 1981 and purchased the real estate office from Joseph E. Uncle in 1988. At the time, she was the only African American real estate broker in Cape May county.

Preparing the Grill
Whitesboro, New Jersey, 2001

Two men are preparing food for the 11th Annual Whitesboro
Community Reunion.

ChaNice Matthews
Whitesboro, New Jersey, 2002

ChaNice sits patiently while her sister Latoya braids her hair.

Gladys Spaulding
Whitesboro, New Jersey, 1989

Gladys Spaulding is the daughter-in-law of Henry Spaulding. Henry and Hattie Spaulding, along with their son Theodore, were among the first residents of Whitesboro.

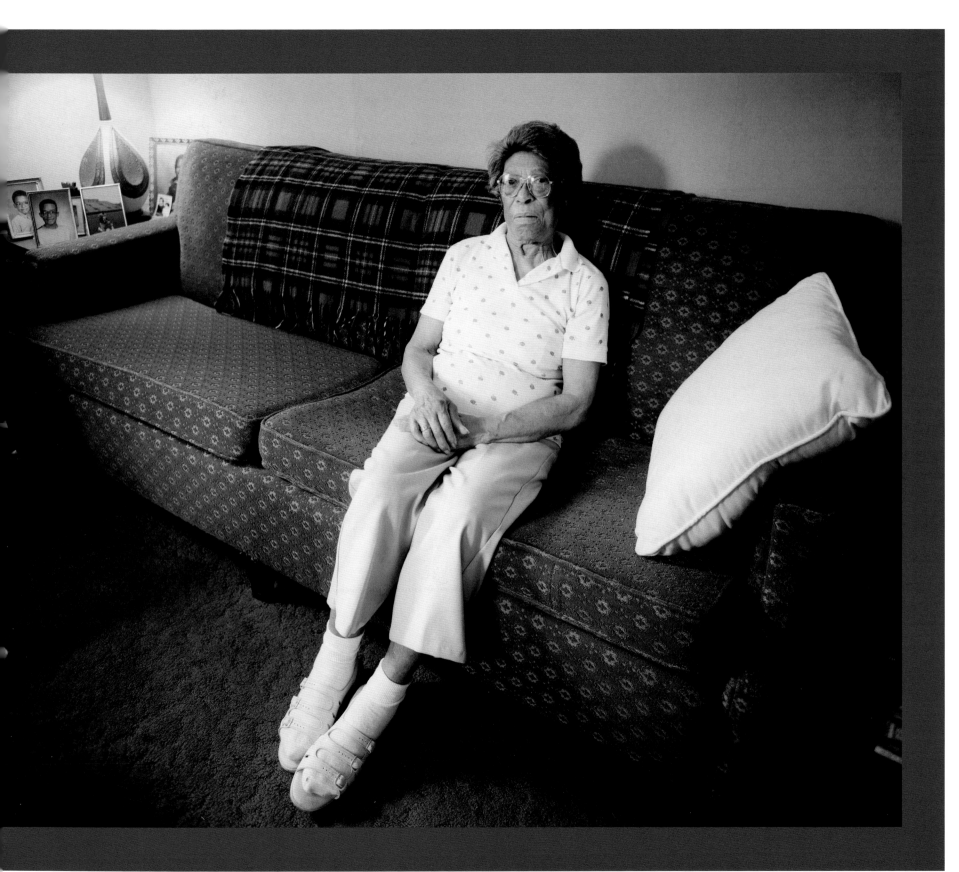

Male-Tones Gospel Singers
Whitesboro, New Jersey, 1989

Four members of the Male-Tones, at the First Baptist Church. From the left the members are Paul Reynolds, Johnnie Richardson, Tommy Wise and William Halliburton.

Alice Jones
Whitesboro, New Jersey, 1989

Alice Jones (left) moved to Whitesboro in 1907. She was a teacher in the Whitesboro school and one of the longtime residents of the community. Comedian Flip Wilson a one-time Whitesboro resident credited her as the person who helped to motivate him. Mrs. Jones died August 1991.

Paul Reynolds
President, Male-Tones Gospel Singers
Whitesboro, New Jersey, 1989

Paul Reynolds moved to Whitesboro in 1965 with his wife, Mary Ruth. Mrs. Reynolds died in 1984; her funeral was on the day of their fifty-first anniversary.

Re-Focus on Our Youth!!
Whitesboro, New Jersey, 2001

A Whitesboro resident (background) wearing a t-shirt
announcing the theme of the 11th Annual Reunion—
Re-Focus on Our Youth!!

Three Girls
Whitesboro, New Jersey, 1989

Three girls wait patiently for activities during the Whitesboro Community Reunion at the Martin Luther King, Jr., Recreation Center.

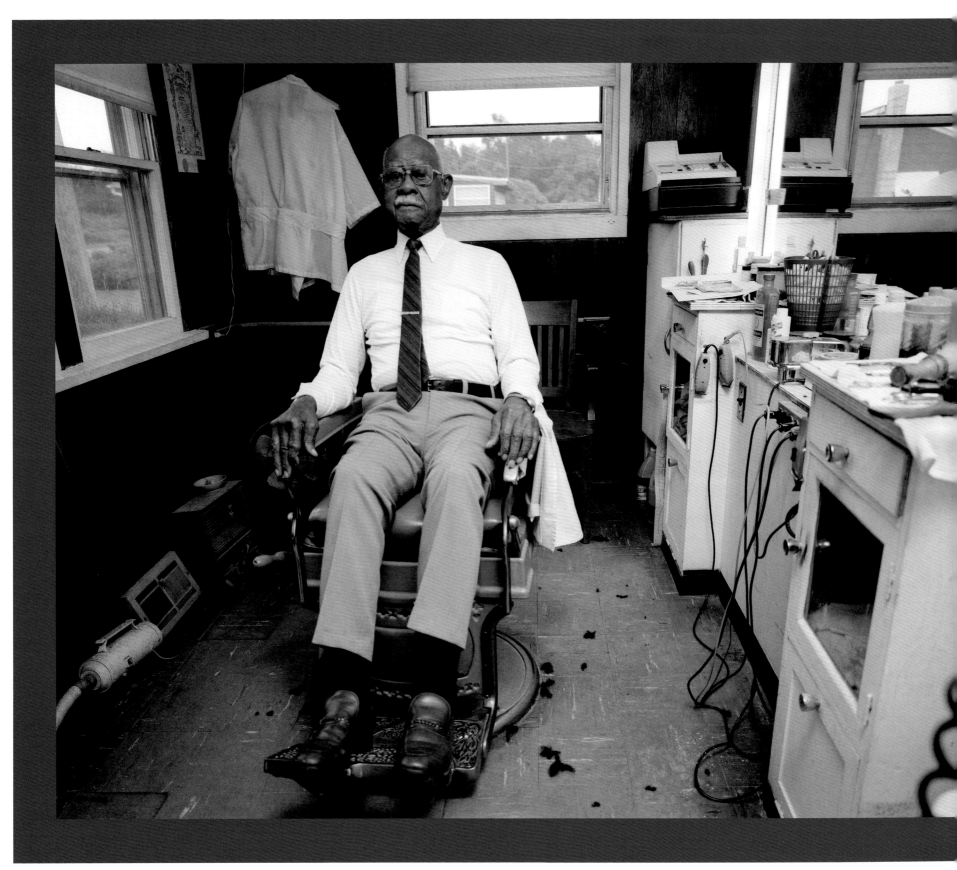

Woodie Armstrong's Barbershop
Whitesboro, New Jersey, 1989

Woodie Armstrong recalled childhood memories from
North Carolina of Congressman George H. White,
founder of Whitesboro. Mr. Armstrong visited Whitesboro
many times before he retired in 1958, moved to
Whitesboro, and opened a barbershop in his home.

Whitesboro Head Start
Whitesboro, New Jersey, 1990

Site of the first church and one-room school started in 1904. The Head Start building was originally constructed by Middle Township to serve Whitesboro as a "separate but equal" four-room schoolhouse. The first teacher in the original school was Mamie White, daughter of Congressman George H. White.

Near Route 211
Rosindale, North Carolina, 1991

George H. White was born in Rosindale, December 1852. He served as United States Congressman for the 2nd North Carolina district, between 1897 and 1901. In 1899 he (along with others) purchased the property in Cape May County, New Jersey, that would become Whitesboro.

WHITESBORO: A HOMETOWN REMEMBERED

Stedman Graham

When I consider the places I have been and seen, I would consider my hometown of Whitesboro, New Jersey, to be a small town. To describe the small town experience, these words come to mind: fun, challenging, painful, together, class, religious, old-school, depth, anger, pride, needy—and I would end that list with "can't wait to get out."

Growing up in an all-black town within a predominantly white county, we often heard, "nothing good ever comes out of Whitesboro." I recognize now that such a label was intended to make us feel inferior. The programming worked, because I always felt I had to validate myself and prove that I was good enough.

The need to compete for attention was ever-present within the community; we were always trying to outdo each other, particularly when it came to sports. Competition was the process that separated the men from the boys. Our value was based upon our ability to catch a football, run fast, jump high, play basketball, and—above all else—talk trash. As I think back and smile at those times, I wish I could reclaim some of that time and energy to focus on being a better student.

My company specializes in education and training, so I have given some thought to my early years in Whitesboro. Back then, all of the students went to Whitesboro School through the eighth grade; then we moved to Cape May Courthouse, a town three miles from Whitesboro, where for the first time in our lives we attended school with the white kids. The year I entered the fifth grade, the township consolidated and desegregated our community's educational system. Many of the students from the Whitesboro School became very successful professionals. The dropout rate there was much lower than today, even though nowadays they have more technology and resources than ever before. Why was that the case? I've thought about that often. The teachers at our little schoolhouse made sure we were prepared and confident of our skills before we went on to the white school. They understood the challenges we would face when we entered the mainstream and they told us consistently: "You have two strikes against you: you're black and you come from Whitesboro. You've got to be twice as good in everything you do." They made sure we could read, write, and understand math—they gave us the best they could. I would say that a big part of the success of the small-town school was due to the teachers' belief in the possibilities for our futures. They corrected us, kept us in line when we were out of control, and taught us to have self-respect. Many of my class-mates from Whitesboro were very intelligent and some (especially the girls) said with disbelief about the white kids: "I thought they were supposed to be so smart." However, the message from the surrounding white communities was still based on the assumption of black inferiority. Because we were trying so hard to be like white Americans, our sense of self-respect suffered, and as a result we often perceived ourselves as "less than." Not withstanding the history of African Americans in professional sports, the athletic arena offered a form of opportunity and equality, so as a result we often prevailed because we were expected to excel. With sports, we could create self-esteem without interference.

Race was an important topic in our town. It defined our daily experiences. Racism was so all-consuming that we even classified ourselves based on the shades of our complexions. I was deeply affected by this class system. My family background is a multi-ethnic mix of African American, Native American, and Scottish American. As light-skinned people, we were convinced to feel superior to those with a darker complexion. This attitude, based on skin color, was detrimental to me and to many others in my family, who felt the same way—because our focus was on the external features instead of on strengthening our knowledge and community. I walked around with a feeling of entitlement—which many of my white brothers and sisters have— that is very dangerous, because it hinders self-awareness and personal growth.

When I look back on my life, I realize that living in our wonderful town, we had only limited power and influence. Although some residents of Whitesboro—including my father—owned businesses, we didn't really have direct control over our lives, especially with respect to political representation or influence. This was one of the most tragic consequences for our town, because the needs of the community were mostly neglected and marginalized: we were not even in the game.

What was wonderful throughout those early years before integration, was that we were embraced by our community and within Whitesboro, and we felt safe. So much so that if you were not from the "Boro," as we called it, you were at risk. That has changed quite a bit now. But in those days, there was a bond among all of us who were from Whitesboro, because we all felt the same pain. Many of us left town in order to achieve various personal and professional goals. Some stayed and continue to lead successful and productive lives, others moved away and later returned—but unfortunately, too many are in jail, lost on drugs, or dead.

I remember my group of classmates and friends as being full of so much talent and raw skill. Many were smarter and more talented than me, but some were destroyed by the image created for them or by not feeling worthy, valued, or by not understanding the process for development and having a greater vision for themselves. In this small town in New Jersey, we were all of the same people seeking common goals—love and validation. But we allowed our lives to become routine doing the same thing over and over, every day. What have we done? We never got to turn the brain on. We lost the ability to think productively because we were programmed to follow the definitions of others, failing to develop either as individuals or as a community.

Freedom is about understanding potential and being able to think, create, build, and develop that potential to its highest level utilizing the available resources. In Whitesboro we experienced a form of freedom as long as we stayed within our community. As we ventured out, many of us were under the impression that we didn't have the ability to transfer that sense of freedom and confidence to the outside world. I was fortunate to discover for myself a means to heal that hole in my heart that I carried for so many years. I was able to free myself from the pain—peeling the onion and get down to the core—to rebuild myself, creating a life based on knowledge and positive images. It is a wonderful feeling. So much so, I wrote about it in a book, *You Can Make It Happen: A Nine-Step Plan for Success*.

Whitesboro is a special place to me. It is part of my legacy. There are so many fond memories and I owe it a great deal of gratitude. The spirit and personality of the people, teachers, and church leaders are with me every day in my conversations, in my clarity and comments, in my lectures and speaking, in my relationships, in the board meetings, and in my profession and business. I hope other people who read this will be able to relate to the experiences and benefits of being raised in a small town and the great effect it had on black lives.

Franklin Street School
Cape May, New Jersey, 2002

The Franklin Street School in Cape May opened in 1927 and functioned as a "separate but equal" elementary school in Cape May until 1948. It may have been one of the last segregated schools in the state. On May 17, 1997, community groups sponsored a reunion, attended by many of the former students.

Franklin Street School Classroom
Cape May, New Jersey, 2002

Interior of the Franklin Street School. The
blackboard/moveable partition is in the upstairs classroom.

Classroom window, Franklin Street School, Cape May, New Jersey, 2001

Franklin Street School
Cape May, New Jersey, 1996

Front doors of the Franklin Street School in Cape May.
Originally a part of the segregated school system in New
Jersey, the building has served as a municipal storage area.
The city plans to restore the building as a cultural and
arts center.

Clinton
Shiloh Seeley
Roadstown o Bowen
Sheppards Mill
Greenwich
Bacon
C. R. R. of N.
Cohansey
Caviar P. O. or
Bayside Sta.
Cedar

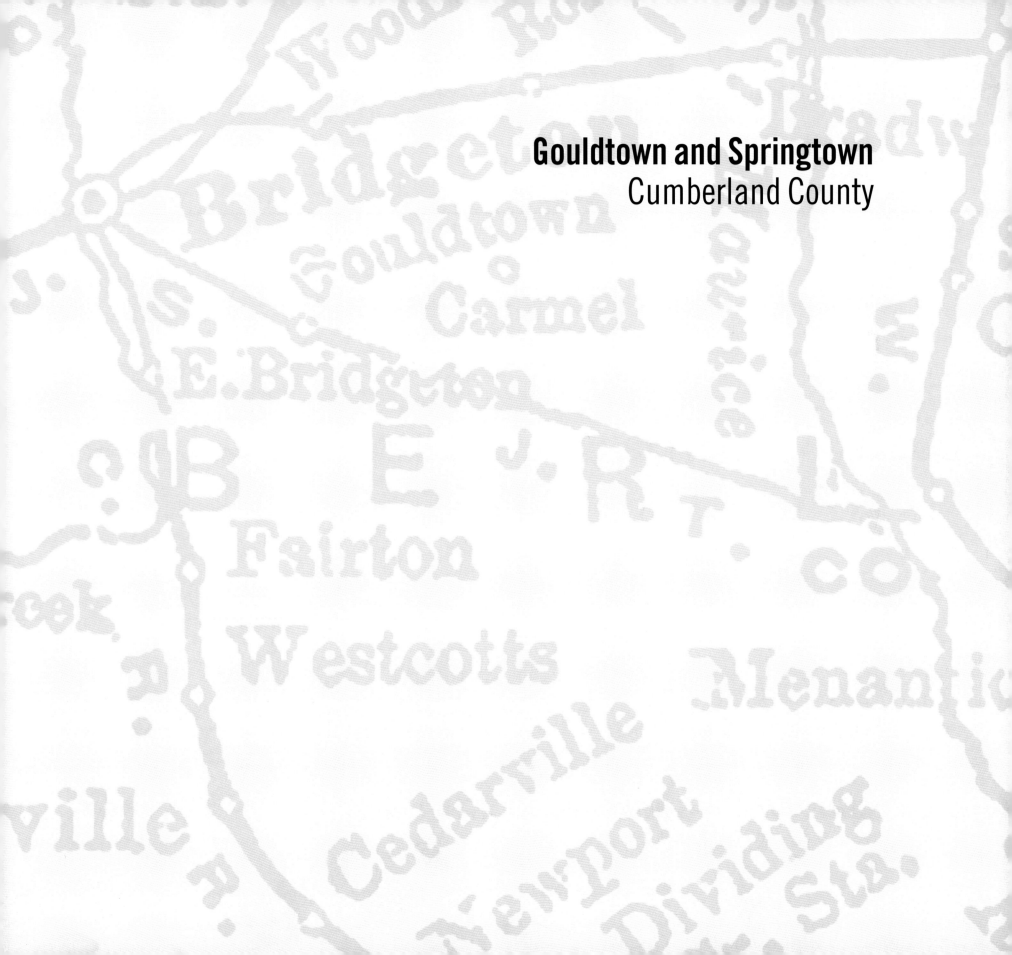

Gouldtown and Springtown
Cumberland County

Trinity A.M.E. Church
Gouldtown, New Jersey, 1993

In his 1913 book, *Gouldtown: A Very Remarkable Settlement of Ancient Date*, William Steward quotes Judge Lucius Elmer's 1865 history of Cumberland County: "Gouldtown—partly in the Northern part of Fairfield, and partly in Bridgeton Townships—although never more than a settlement of mulattoes, principally bearing the names of Gould and Pierce, scattered over a considerable territory, is of quite ancient date."

Bethel A.M.E. Church
Springtown, New Jersey, 2002

The Bethel A.M.E. Church was established in 1810, most likely at a nearby location in Greenwich, New Jersey—on the site of the Ambury Hill cemetery. In both the current and previous locations the church was a station in the Underground Railroad.

Laura Aldridge
Bethel A.M.E. Church
Springtown, New Jersey, 2002

Laura Aldridge did not grow up in Springtown, however as a child she attended the Bethel A.M.E. Church every Sunday with her mother, whose family, the Bryants were longtime residents of Springtown. She became involved with the preservation and restoration of the church as outgrowth of working on a family genealogy.

Interior, Bethel A.M.E. Church, Springtown, New Jersey, 2002

United Methodist Church
Springtown, New Jersey, 2000

The United Methodist Church is no longer in use. There is a small African American cemetery on the side of the church.

Springtown, New Jersey, 1999

View of the original location of the natural spring that provided the name for this early nineteenth-century black community.

Small Gloucester, Swedesboro and Elsmere
Gloucester County

Mount Zion A.M.E. Church
Small Gloucester, New Jersey, 1998

This image was made just before the 1999 bicentennial celebration of the establishment of this congregation in what was once a black settlement outside the town of Swedesboro. The congregation joined the A.M.E. conference in 1816 and the current structure was built in 1834. The church and its members served the Underground Railroad.

Mount Zion A.M.E. Cemetery
Small Gloucester, New Jersey, 1998

Before the cleanup, Mount Zion cemetery was inaccessible due to overgrowth and construction debris. Here the headstone of Viola P. Finnaman is hidden beneath discarded lumber.

Viola P. Finnaman Grave
Mount Zion A.M.E. Cemetery
Small Gloucester, New Jersey, 2002

This headstone marking the grave of Viola P. Finnaman was covered with debris and obscured by overgrowth before the efforts to restore and preserve the cemetery. Mount Zion Church was part of the New Jersey Underground Railroad.

Exterior view of Mount Zion A.M.E. Cemetery, Small Gloucester, New Jersey, 2002

Re-dedication Ceremony
Mount Zion A.M.E. Church
Small Gloucester, New Jersey, 2001

Members of a Civil War historical interpretation group set
up a campsite and educational displays for the community
as part of the re-dedication ceremony.

Fredric Minus
Mount Zion A.M.E. Church
Small Gloucester, New Jersey, 2001

After the ceremony re-dedicating the Mount Zion
cemetery, Fredric Minus discusses the role of black soldiers
during the Civil War.

Elaine Edwards and Sarah Lucile Stewart-Mitchell
Swedesboro, New Jersey, 2001

Elaine Edwards and Lucile Stewart-Mitchell are standing in the Mount Lebanon Lodge that once served as the one-room segregated school for this community. Mrs. Edwards and Mrs. Stewart-Mitchell worked to have this building listed on the state and national historic registries.

Richardson Avenue School
Swedesboro, New Jersey, 1999

The Mount Lebanon Lodge Masonic Hall on Richardson Avenue served as a "separate but equal" school from 1931 until 1942. The Richardson Avenue School is listed in the New Jersey Register of Historic Places and the National Register of Historic Places.

Robert Tucker
Elsmere, New Jersey, 2002

Robert Tucker is an active civic leader and community historian. Originally from Elsmere, his family moved several times during his childhood but finally returned to this community. Having undergraduate and graduate degrees in chemistry, Mr. Tucker was teacher, guidance counselor, and superintendent of schools in Lawnside, New Jersey. Involved with NAACP, he teaches photography to teens.

Mount Moriah Primitive Baptist Church
Elsmere, New Jersey, 2002

Elsmere, at one time called Eighty Acres, was created as a black settlement for one of the glassworks in the area. During the late 1930s, Arthur Rothstein photographed the community while working for the FSA.

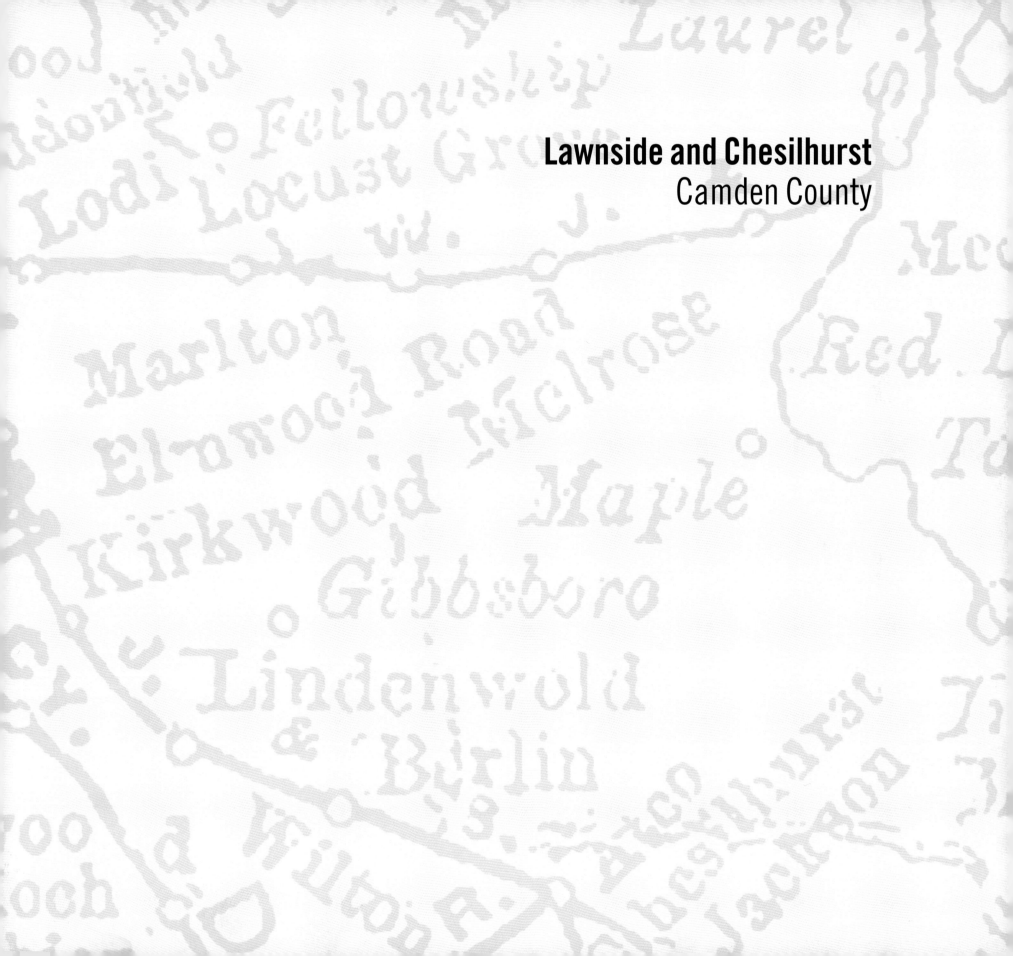

Lawnside and Chesilhurst
Camden County

Clarence Still
Lawnside, New Jersey, 2001

Clarence Still is a descendant of the original settlers of the community that would eventually become Lawnside. He worked with others in the community to save and preserve the Peter Mott House—a station on the Underground Railroad.

Peter Mott House
Lawnside, New Jersey, 2001

Elaine Edwards (pointing), Linda Waller, and Sarah Lucile Stewart-Mitchell at the dedication of the remodeled Peter Mott House.

Peter Mott House
Lawnside, New Jersey, 2001

Guests and members of the community tour the newly restored Peter Mott House after the dedication ceremony.

Dedication of Peter Mott House
Lawnside, New Jersey, 2001

Linda Waller (center, facing camera) is president of the Lawnside Historical Society. The audience is gathered for the beginning of the dedication ceremony for the Peter Mott House.

Mount Peace Cemetery
Lawnside, New Jersey, 2001

The Civil War graves in the Mount Peace cemetery. In one section of the cemetery two rows of headstones mark the graves of Civil War veterans, though not all had been residents of the Lawnside community.

Gloria Miller, Alexis Dabney, and Pamela Miller Dabney
Carl Miller Funeral Home
Lawnside, New Jersey, 2002

Pamela Miller Dabney (foreground) and her brother Carl are the fifth generation of the Miller family to work in the funeral business. Seated behind her are her mother and daughter (who is currently an intern working toward a license and will be the sixth generation in the funeral business.) The Miller family has been in the Lawnside area since before the Civil War. Carl Miller, Sr. (Pamela's grandfather) received a license in 1927 and moved his family and the funeral business from nearby Magnolia to Lawnside in 1934. His grandmother, Leah Frances Miller, started the funeral business in 1861 in Magnolia, New Jersey.

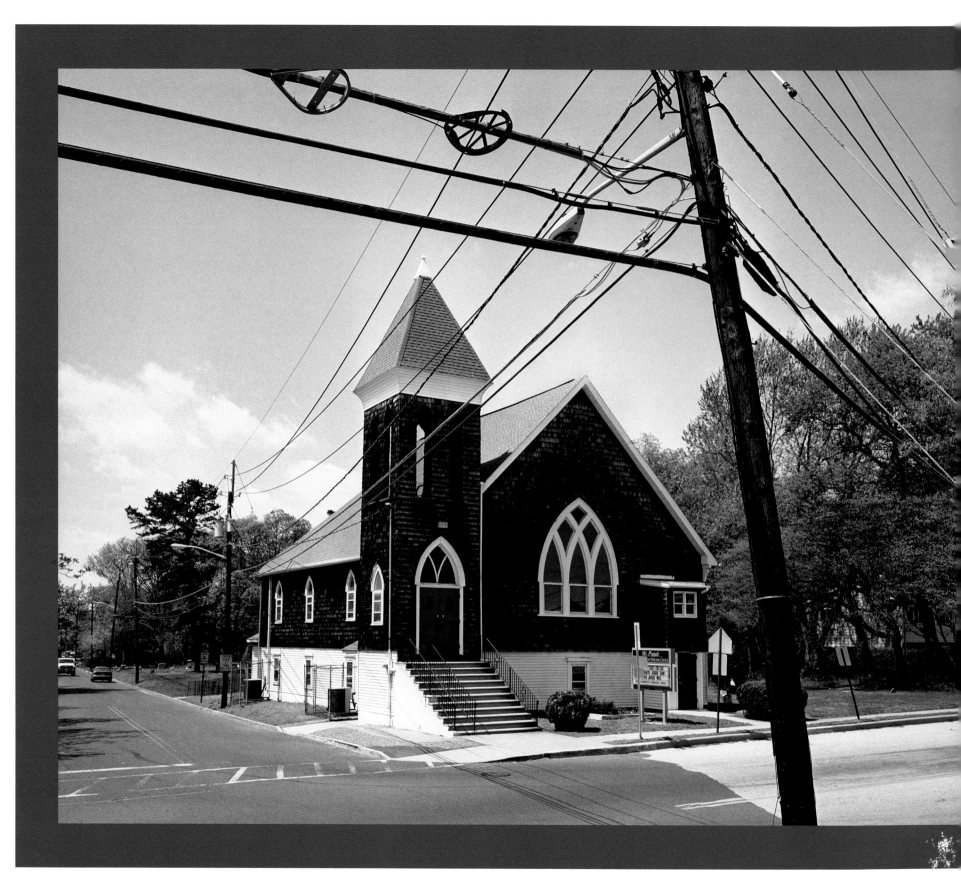

Mount Pisgah A.M.E. Church
Lawnside, New Jersey, 2002

Mount Pisgah A.M.E. Church is one of the oldest A.M.E. churches in southern New Jersey. It was established by Bishop Richard Allen, founder of the A.M.E. church and it is the burial site for Jareena Lee, the first female preacher in the church.

Lawnside Roll of Honor, Lawnside, New Jersey, 2002

Chesilhurst Boro Hall
Chesilhurst, New Jersey, 1993

The Boro Hall is centrally located on Grant Ave. Arland
Poindexter was mayor of Chesilhurst.

Mayor Arland Poindexter
Chesilhurst, New Jersey, 1992

Arland Poindexter was born in 1943 in Philadelphia and moved to Chesilhurst in 1969. After serving as a member of the town council for six years, Mr. Poindexter was elected mayor of Chesilhurst in 1986. He and his wife, Pricilla, have two sons.

Dr. Merrie Hill
Chesilhurst, New Jersey, 1993

Dr. Merrie Hill was born in Cleveland, Ohio, and moved to Chesilhurst in 1986. The property was originally purchased in 1958 by her uncle, Alvin Williams. Dr. Hill studied at the New England Conservatory of Music and in 1982 received a doctorate in education from Temple University.

Grant A.M.E. Church
Chesilhurst, New Jersey, c. 1950

The lots for this church were purchased in 1886 and the original building was constructed in 1888. This image, from the church archive, shows a structure dedicated in 1936; the current building was dedicated in 1973.

Grant A.M.E. Church Office
Chesilhurst, New Jersey, 1993

The original church organ, now in storage, was built by the
Esty Organ Company in Brattleboro, Vermont. Purchased
near the end of the nineteenth or beginning of the
twentieth century, it was used in the old church building.

Cemetery
Chesilhurst, New Jersey, 1993

Headstone in the African American cemetery on Grant
Ave. The graves are not visible from the road.

First Baptist Church, Chesilhurst, New Jersey, 1993

Pleasant Harrison
Chesilhurst, New Jersey, 1994

Pleasant Harrison was born in Branchville, South Carolina and married Eddie Harrison in 1935. She purchased property in Chesilhurst in 1949. In 1961 she began to build her home—built almost entirely by herself—and completed it in 1963.

Reverend James Saylor
Chesilhurst, New Jersey, 1993

James Saylor was born in Ashville, North Carolina, and he moved to Chesilhurst in 1963. He became custodian of the Chesilhurst School in 1976 and has been pastor of Mount Zion Baptist Church in Weymouth, New Jersey, since 1989. Reverend Saylor is married with four children.

Tecolia Salters
West Atco, New Jersey, 1994

Tecolia Salters was born in Cross Anchor, South Carolina, and married Emanuel Salters in 1942. In 1959 they moved to this home, just outside Chesilhurst, with five acres cultivated as a produce and poultry farm. Although the Salters were employed, they continued to farm, and sold produce in Philadelphia on weekends. Mr. Salters died in April 1991.

Map

- Zontown
- Malaga
- Newfield
- Forest Grove
- Cedar Lake
- Hebron
- Newto[n]
- Wheat Road
- Piantola F. R. R.
- Landisville
- Maine Ave
- Buena
- Richland
- Vineland
- S. Vineland
- Clayville
- Creek

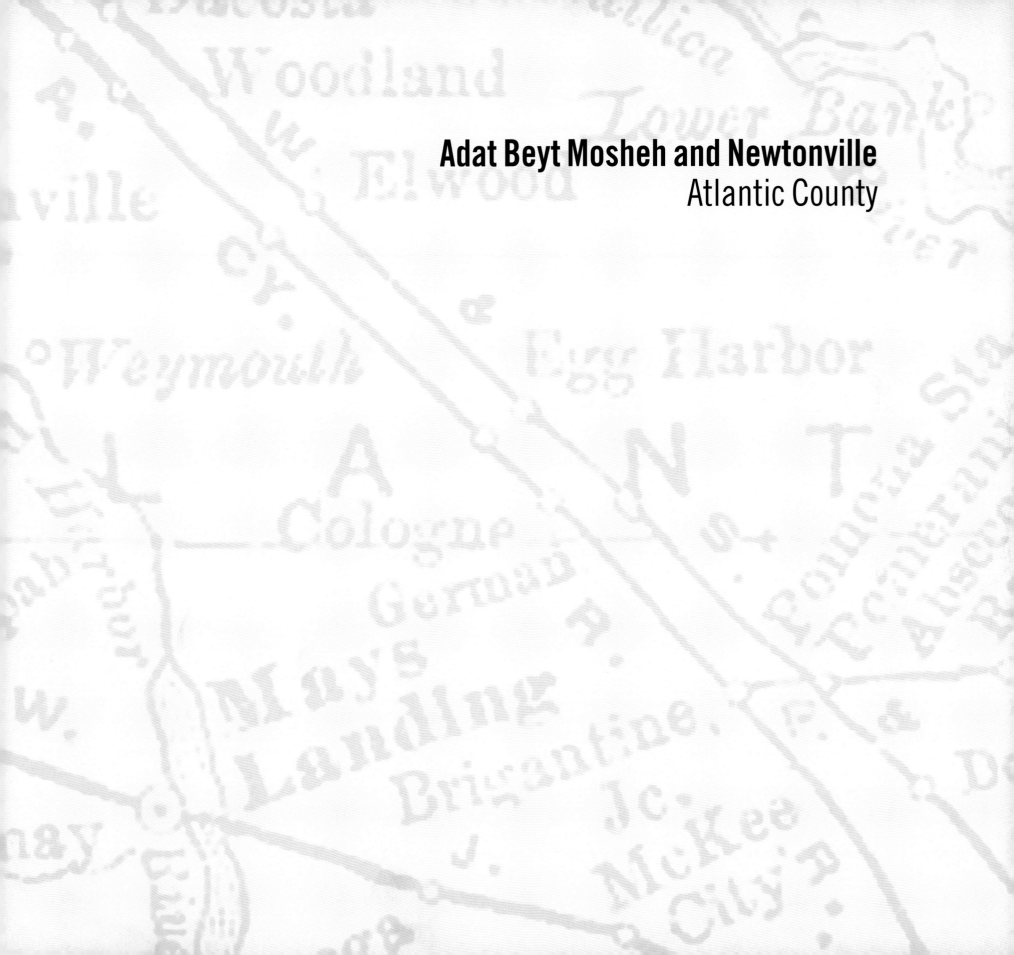

Adat Beyt Mosheh and Newtonville
Atlantic County

Adat Beyt Mosheh Congregation
Near Elwood, New Jersey, 2002

Adat Beyt Mosheh is the spiritual and social center of this community of Jews of color. In a brochure printed in 1962 its founder, Sar Abel Respes, calls Adat Beyt Mosheh "America's Colored Hebrew Community." The congregation formed in Philadelphia in 1951 and moved to southern New Jersey in 1962. The foreword to the 1962 brochure describes the community: "The homes are the most modern construction, totally electric, situated in an ideal rural area just off the White Horse Pike, bounded on all sides by an abundance of beautiful green trees and lawns, within a healthful area where sunshine and fresh air are plentiful, the water unpolluted, and quiescence is constantly prevalent. The absence of industrial plants and factories are a safeguard against air-pollution."

Adat Beyt Mosheh Community
Near Elwood, New Jersey, 2002

Four of the five homes that are part of a black Jewish community founded by Rabbi Sar Abel Respes. Clockwise from upper right are the homes of some of his children and grandchildren—Gabrielle, Anita (died February 2002), and Elkanah. In the upper left is the home of Manuel.

Adat Beyt Mosheh
Near Elwood, New Jersey, 2002

The home of Rabbi Abel Respes and his wife, Viola, which they built as the center of the Adat Beyt Mosheh community. The current residents are his children Diane, Mosheh, and Eliyahu.

Respes Family in Adat Beyt Mosheh
Near Elwood, New Jersey, 2002

Members of the Respes family inside the temple Adat Beyt Mosheh. In the top row are three of Abel Respes' sons: Mosheh (left), Manuel, and Eliyahu. Abel and Viola Respes had twenty-one children: Anita, Diane, Alender, Gabrielle, Abel, Judy, Joel, Leah, Elkanah, Tirzah, Mosheh, Gamaiel, Zayith, Manuel, Keturah, Michal, Ben Yamin, Miriam, Eliyahu, Hadassah, and Gila.

Dugout House
Newtonville, New Jersey, 2001

Remains of a "dugout" home in Newtonville. The dugout house method was used in rural southern New Jersey as an inexpensive form of home construction. The occupants would excavate the basement (dugout) and build the foundation, cover it with roofing material, and begin to live in the site. Later, with more funds, the rest of the house was added above. This home was owned and lived in by Reverend Warren during the 1960s—but the upper portion was not completed before he died.

Michelle Washington Wilson
Newtonville, New Jersey, 2001

Michelle Wilson is a storyteller, motivational speaker, college recruiter, and educator. She is seated in the ruins of her childhood home located on what is still a dirt road in Newtonville, New Jersey.

Cemetery
Newtonville, New Jersey, 1995

Grave marker in one of the Newtonville cemeteries that reflects African traditions. Some graves are marked with found or significant objects and others have traditional headstones.

HOME AND HEARTH:
THE BLACK TOWN AND SETTLEMENT MOVEMENT OF SOUTHERN NEW JERSEY

Clement Alexander Price

The old town, where home and hearth are protected and well remembered, is among the most powerfully sentimental images in America. Indeed, the town, village, hamlet, enclave, and other small living places have sustained, perhaps as much as anything else in the American imagination, an enduring belief in the nation's peaceful isolation in an otherwise troubled world. Such places and the memories they bring forth are sources of the nation's belief in its exceptionalism.

During the nineteenth century, when the irrepressible cadence of industrialization and the growth of cities increasingly challenged the supremacy of agrarian America, the small town became a prominent feature in the nation's image of its former self. The famous lithographers Currier and Ives, as an example, romanticized it in their sentimental images of an American landscape that was crossing the threshold into a new and uncertain industrial age. In the second half of twentieth century, the American illustrator and painter Norman Rockwell burnished our nostalgia for small-town America at a time when most Americans lived within burgeoning metropolitan areas. Towns, many Americans believed, were the nexus of the better part of the nation's values and culture, the middle ground in our collective consciousness about community and public and private life. Having some of the admirable features of urban life—most notably a concentration of social energy, commerce, and ritual—

towns also satisfied America's romantic attachment to the countryside and its assumed characteristics of individualism, homogeneity, safety, and stability.

Until recently the towns planned, laid out, and settled by blacks have been largely left out of this portrait of American fortitude, community values, and quiet progress. Most Americans know of black towns and settlements through popular images on film, in which black residents seemed destined to be attacked by mobs of whites, their buildings burned to the ground, and, finally, to be run out of town. Some black towns and their residents indeed suffered that awful fate in the twentieth century, but most did not. More often towns founded by blacks survived until their residents pursued a fuller measure of progress and opportunity in other towns and cities. But as Wendel White's photographs in this volume show, some of these black towns still survive.

Fortunately, efforts by nineteenth- and twentieth-century blacks to establish communities of various sizes and degrees of complexity have not been totally forgotten. The older residents of such places have become instrumental in aiding photographers, journalists, historians, and filmmakers in discovering a past that had been nearly obscured by our fascination with the present and the future.[1] These town elders, many of whom are the progeny of the founders, have safeguarded the stories of their families. At a time when Americans are taking a greater interest in their past, African Americans are especially passionate about their local and regional history. Many now comprehend how the Civil Rights movement and desegregation affected traditional African American community life. Many blacks want to know more of what their forebears accomplished under the long shadows cast by Jim Crow.

Segregation should not to be romanticized; it certainly must never again become a way of life accepted by law and custom. And yet over the years that many African Americans lived in separate places within a larger racial caste system, they displayed a tenacity of purpose that is instructive for our own times. What they accomplished in the face of considerable odds in the two generations following the Great Emancipation was remarkable. They built churches and organizations that served as centers of spiritual comfort and moral guidance. They started fraternal orders that fostered socialization and civic work. Preserving the centrality of music in the black community, they founded myriad singing ensembles that promoted musical literacy and reverence for both the African American vernacular and European classical traditions of music.[2] They formed baseball teams that helped to modernize entertainment in the black community while promoting athleticism and what the social activist and literary artist Amiri Baraka has called "public ritual." They launched businesses that catered almost exclusively to black patrons in need of personal care, real estate, banking, legal assistance, photography, carpentry and construction, and funeral services. They started newspapers that discouraged gossip while providing information and context for contemporary events. And during those years, in growing numbers, black children in New Jersey entered schools, all but ending illiteracy. Black towns were central to these developments in the years following the Great Emancipation.

For that reason scholars now hold considerable interest in the daily life of these places that blacks created for themselves. *Small Towns, Black Lives* illuminates the legacies of these traditional aspects of black life in the northern states, specifically the rich African American historical and cultural terrain of South Jersey.

Black towns in the southern counties of New Jersey emerged principally during the second half of the nineteenth century. Their early history mirrors circumstances resulting from the intersection of race and place in the United States.[3] At mid-century, free blacks in the northern states lived in areas perceived by whites to be inferior and less desirable. Indeed, in many American towns and cities blacks were sequestered in districts where infamy was thought to exist. At the same time, white racial hostility convinced many blacks of the need to settle in places where they would be left alone. In many of these areas blacks laid the foundation, as best they could, for their lives as free people. In such places inhabited by blacks, where poverty and racism defined the social status of the race, they took the early steps toward group agency, autonomy, and preservation.[4]

The black town movement became all the more intense in the last decades of the nineteenth century, when racial feelings and aspirations in America ran high on both sides of the color line. After the end of Reconstruction, whites in the northern and southern states increasingly condoned efforts by racial supremacists to subjugate blacks in civil, social, and economic matters. By the end of the century racial segregation was a way of life in the

United States, as society became all the more racialized from an effort by the dominant white population to thwart endeavors by blacks to compete politically, economically, or socially in modern America. Black leaders realized the limitations imposed on members of their race by a society that denied equal constitutional rights and fair entry into the marketplace. They also realized that slavery's end presented new opportunities. Separate towns, schools, and religious and secular organizations were envisioned as ways to protect the race's vulnerable interests, reflecting the larger emphasis on black uplift through institutional development during the age of Booker T. Washington.

New Jersey had a unique relationship with this man from Tuskegee, Alabama. As the most influential black leader at the turn of the twentieth century, Washington exerted much influence over modern African American politics, education, and ideology, especially in New Jersey, where his views may have had a greater resonance than in any other northern state. He visited the state on more than a few occasions, seeking support for his beloved Tuskegee Institute in Alabama as well as endorsements of his ideas for Negro uplift. During the early twentieth century, scores of his colleagues and protégés settled or launched projects in New Jersey, including George Henry White, the founder of Whitesboro. In keeping with the Tuskegee Institute model, New Jersey's Washingtonians began organizations that catered almost exclusively to black patrons, serving as well as emblems of respectability and progress. Black towns, which Washington supported, were in keeping with the prevailing belief of some contemporaries—that the race could profit from separation.

Clearly, one of Washington's most important legacies in New Jersey, and a corollary of the black town movement, was the Bordentown Manual Training and Industrial School for Colored Youth. Founded in 1886 as the Technical Industrial Educational Association of New Brunswick, the

Bordentown School was modeled after the better-known school in Tuskegee. For seventy years, it educated black girls and boys from across the state. Not unlike black towns, it was a source of considerable pride in black New Jersey. Bordentown also aroused the consternation of black leaders who saw it, perhaps all too simply, as a state-supported manifestation of Jim Crow practices in public education. Those opposed to the school prevailed: it was closed in 1955. Changing perceptions of black life in New Jersey and beyond, and the rising tide of civil rights activism, brought into question the continued value of a black educational institution.

   Black towns and settlements were also inspired by quasi-utopian religious sects in nineteenth-century America that devoted themselves to the building and preservation of their own communities. Black men and women, perhaps seeking to replicate such efforts, sought to give their towns and settlements a symbolic importance within the optimistic framework of American society. In such a place it was possible for nineteenth-century ideals and premises—the domesticity of women, masculine authority in the home, home ownership, a sturdy work ethic, and amelioration of vice and criminality—to gain traction. Living beyond the scrutiny of strangers, blacks in their towns and settlements could also engage in rituals informed by their own cultural traditions. In these places they could enjoy fealty from members of their ethnic group, those who shared the common experience of suffering and hope. To an extent, then, and on their own terms, black settlements contributed to the belief in African American exceptionalism.

   New Jersey's important and unique role in the national movement that led to the formation of exclusively black towns and communities is well captured by Wendel White's rich array of photographs and text. Historians have provided a chronological context and interpretation of such places, but their imagery of past narratives has been less evident. Not many years ago, in 1994,

Morris Beach, New Jersey

a photographic exhibition on black historic life in Morris County was mounted, and over the following years there have been other presentations that depict the history and memory of Negro sports in the state, business culture, religious institutions, and communal life. Wendel White's visual documentation of black life in southern New Jersey sustains such work, but it is also a major breakthrough in that for the first time it illuminates more than two generations of historical scholarship revealed previously only in words.

Beginning in 1941, with Marion Thompson Wright's magnum opus, *Education of Negroes in New Jersey*,[5] we have known that America's most powerful metaphors—blackness and whiteness—marked social, civic, and political realities and inequalities in New Jersey, especially in the nineteenth century and well into the twentieth. New Jersey's geographical proximity to the South's peculiar institution of slavery, and indeed the state's own longtime enslavement of blacks, influenced the way blacks and whites interacted and how they viewed themselves and each other. Indeed, New Jersey's location so close to the Mason-Dixon Line fostered a border state mentality on racial matters.

The state's white population embraced liberal racial and cultural views that were more characteristic of the North. There were, for example, abolitionist sentiments and activities in New Jersey, especially as the nineteenth century unfolded and as the indignities of slavery in the South and in other parts of the Americas became more widely known. The more fortunate blacks in the state held property, started businesses that were patronized by a cross-section of their neighbors and, in some cases, were treated with respect. From the early nineteenth century blacks were accorded schooling and, in 1881, the New Jersey Legislature passed a law that forbade the exclusion of children from public schools because of religion, nationality, or color. Although the bill was poorly enforced, especially in the southern counties, it nevertheless gave blacks the confidence and foundation upon which to argue their civil rights in the years ahead.[6]

Still, New Jersey's black communities faced obstacles to their viability. Incidences of violence against blacks in the nineteenth and twentieth centuries have been documented; race demarcated public life in the formal and informal use of space and institutions. As noted earlier, this was especially the case in public schools, which were racially segregated in the southern counties until the 1940s and, in some cases, until after the New Jersey State Constitution of 1947 mandated the end of the practice.

If New Jersey's complicated racial customs encouraged the formation of black towns and settlements, the same may be said to result from the state's geography. Over the course of the nineteenth century, New Jersey was one of the variegated passageways for blacks escaping slavery in the south along the Underground Railroad. Giles R. Wright has persuasively argued that "no other northern state exceeded New Jersey in the number of all-black communities that served the as UGRR sanctuaries for southern fugitive slaves."[7] Southern New Jersey's provincial character and vast expanse of largely unsettled land may also have enabled runaway slaves to establish safe havens.

The earliest of the towns for which artifactual and documentary evidence exists is Gouldtown. Located in Fairfield Township, Cumberland County, its early inhabitants were of mixed racial heritage, including descendants of Benjamin Gould, a man of African ancestry, and his Anglo-American wife, Elizabeth Adams. Other early towns included Springtown, in Greenwich Township, Cumberland County. Its settlers were escaped slaves whose legacies in memory, institutions, and structures were sustained by their progeny. One of the earliest settlers of the community, Levin Steel, came to Springtown from Maryland's Eastern Shore. Significantly, Steel, who changed his surname to Still, was the father of William Still, the great chronicler of the Underground Railroad, and Dr. James Still, a folk healer in the New Jersey Pinelands who was arguably the most prominent New Jersey resident of African ancestry in the waning years of the nineteenth century.[8]

In Camden County, beginning in the eighteenth century, and later during the years that preceded the Civil War, free blacks in the North and southern slaves making their way north settled in a place called Snowhill. Over the following years it became known as Free Haven and, in 1887, Lawnside. It still exists. Not unlike Whitesboro in Cape May County, Lawnside was a planned community. But unlike most black towns in the nation, it was incorporated in 1926, one of the nation's few black settlements so designated.[9] Atlantic County's Port Republic and Morris Beach, Gloucester County's Small Gloucester, Burlington County's Timbuctoo, and Camden County's Chesilhurst, were smaller areas of black settlement. Less well known, they are nevertheless significant in our understanding of African American history and culture in southern New Jersey. Scholars of the black experience have shown that in such enclaves traditions were tenacious because of the near isolation of their residents. Folkways remained strong in these rural communities, manifested in religious organizations, burial grounds, husbandry, and in many other daily routines that hearkened back to distant cultural antecedents in America, the Caribbean and, to be sure, West Africa.

America's racial hierarchy designated these places as black towns in the cultural imagination of New Jersey and the nation. Their cultural identity and history, however, was far more complicated. Social class and color also played a role in their history. Gouldtown, for example, was a racially nuanced community for settlers of interracial heritage. Color mattered in a society where lighter skin enabled some blacks to socially differentiate themselves from others of darker hue. Lightness of skin often coincided with educational advancement, self-confidence, and deference from whites. Homogeneity was revealed in ways other than color, however. In some towns, settlers shared the common experience of having escaped from slavery in the South, or having derived from the same place. Undoubtedly, though, black racial solidarity and fealty gave the towns their sense of purpose.

Black towns, including those in which a person's lighter skin color seemingly conferred upon them and their town a sense of entitlement, helped enrich and sustain modern black life. In these places familial customs, racial chauvinism, and the credo of American progress converged. Their success or failure was a reflection of the determination and good fortune of their founders and settlers. Whitesboro, for example, took shape in 1898, after blacks fleeing white racial hostility and violence in Wilmington, North Carolina, settled there. Through the work of the distinguished Negro congressman from North Carolina, George Henry White, Whitesboro became one of the nation's most remarkable black towns. In 1901, White's Afro-American Equitable association purchased the land, which is located in Cape May County, as a place for blacks of "good character, steady and industrious habits."[10]

Whitesboro and Lawnside are remarkable examples of how residents in black towns viewed their future during the years that followed the Great Emancipation. The residents of these towns embraced a credo of group self-reliance and solidarity that enriched local civic pride, purpose, and duty over the many years that led to the Civil Rights movement. In nineteenth- and twentieth-century New Jersey, that credo resonated in virtually every aspect of black life. In public affairs blacks sought to alleviate the burden of segregation, especially in the education of the children. They also fervently created a way of life that harbored their culture, organizations, and beliefs. Forced segregation was demeaning to blacks and they responded often eloquently through petitions, letters, and speeches and through their newspapers and organizations. They sought to build upon the racial separation that custom and law enabled. Over the long years of their protests, blacks in New Jersey, especially in the southern counties, built a world within a world. They created an alternative to the explicit insult of the Jim Crow laws. In education, for example, as Marion Thompson Wright observed, "dissatisfaction [of racial segregation] on the part of Negro citizens made a further contribution to the institution or continuance of separate classes or schools and unequal opportunities for their children."

Always the subject of intense debate within New Jersey's black communities, especially in the southern part of the state, segregation elicited an ambiguous response. It clearly disadvantaged African Americans at a time when the nation's expanding economy, and its ideals, gave white ethnics the opportunity to advance themselves in the society, often at the expense of blacks. As the racial barriers against blacks solidified around the turn of the twentieth century, the social policy and behavior that segregation represented influenced virtually every walk of life. Segregation worked against the aspirations of blacks who sought employment commensurate with their skills and energy. A 1903 study by the Bureau of Statistics of Labor and Industries of New Jersey, for example, revealed a pervasive pattern of discrimination against black laborers in virtually all sectors of the state's industrial economy and the anti-black feelings of recently arrived white immigrants. A New Jersey brick manufacturer in 1903 observed that his company had "no negroes employed at our works and [we] have made no attempt to use negro labor. We prefer, white foreign help such as Hungarians, Polanders, etc." A watch case manufacturer claimed "We do not employ negroes in any capacity, except as porters and laborers." The union representing potters in New Jersey replied "Negroes not admitted, although nothing in the constitution or by-laws forbids their admission. If one were to apply he would be blackballed."[11]

Such attitudes and the practices they countenanced stirred protests against segregation from New Jersey's black leadership. But segregation also encouraged blacks with an entrepreneurial vision—individuals such as George Henry White—to materially develop the separate world into which blacks were being ushered.[12] As the newspaper *Colored American* put it, Whitesboro's settlers were a "colony of Negroes who will live and work by themselves." Towns were ambitious manifestations of that vision of race uplift on common ground. For that reason, the towns and settlements that have survived over the course of the twentieth century are truly historic places. They remind us of the difficult journey that Americans of African ancestry have made since the founding of the Republic. Equally important, these places, in their past and present forms, shed light on the contributions of African Americans to our nation's reverence for freedom, exceptionalism, and the real meaning of safety.

NOTES

1. Films informed by the history and memory of New Jersey African Americans include Tom C. Guy, Jr., *Before You Can Say Jackie Robinson* (1992); Rita Heller, *Chanceman's Brothers & Sisters: The Origins of the 20th Century Morris County Black Community* (1998), and Henry Hampton, *America's War on Poverty, City of Promise* (1995). Recent historical analyses that rely heavily on the oral history of New Jersey African Americans include Wynetta Devore, "The Education of Blacks in New Jersey, 1900-1930: An Exploration in Oral History," (diss. Rutgers University, 1980); Audrey Olsen Faulkner, ed. *When I Was Comin' Up: An Oral History of Aged Blacks*, (Hamden, Conn.: Archon Books, 1982); Cheryl C. Turkington, *Setting Up Our Own City. The Black Community in Morristown. An Oral History* (Morristown, N.J.: Joint Free Library of Morristown and Morris Township, 1993); Henrietta Fuller Robinson and Carolyn Cordelia Williams, *Dedicated to Music: The Legacy of African American Church Musicians and Music Teachers in Southern New Jersey, 1915-1990* (Cherry Hill, N.J.: Africana Homestead Legacy Publishers, 1997).

2. Clement Alexander Price, "Composing the Community, Blacks Making and Teaching Music in Southern New Jersey," in Robinson and Williams, xii-xxi.

3. See David Delaney, *Race, Place, & the Law, 1836–1948* (Austin: University of Texas Press, 1998).

4. See James O. Horton and Lois Horton, *In Hope of Liberty: Culture, Community, and Protest among Northern Free Blacks* (New York: Oxford University Press, 1997).

5. Marion Thompson Wright, *Education of Negroes in New Jersey*

6. L. A. Greene, "A History of African Americans in New Jersey," *Journal of the Rutgers University Library* LVI (June 1994): 35-36.

7. Giles R. Wright, *Steal Away, Steal Away…A Guide to the Underground Railroad in New Jersey* (Trenton: New Jersey Historical Commission, 2001), 3.

8. Clement Alexander Price, ed., *Freedom Not Far Distant: A Documentary History of Afro-Americans in New Jersey* (Newark: New Jersey Historical Society, 1980), 134-136; Giles R. Wright, *Afro-Americans in New Jersey: A Short History* (Trenton: New Jersey Historical Commission, 1988), 38-45. Also, Clement Alexander Price, "We Knew Our Place, We Knew Our Way: Lessons from the Black Past of Southern New Jersey," *Seventh Annual Report of the New Jersey Public Policy Research Institute, Blacks in New Jersey. 1986 Report. A Review of Blacks in South Jersey* (Newark: New Jersey Public Policy Research Institute, 1986).

9. Charles C. Smiley, *The True Story of Lawnside, N.J.* (Camden, N.J., 1921), 32.

10. Benjamin R. Justeen, *George Henry White: An Even Chance in the Race for Life* (Baton Rouge: Louisiana State University Press, 2001), 356–384.

11. Price, *Freedom Not Far Distant*, 204–211.

12. Leonard I. Sweet, *Black Images of America, 1784–1870* (New York: Norton & Company, 1976), 125-147; Nell Irvin Painter, *Standing at Armageddon: The United States, 1877–1919* (New York: Norton & Company, 1987), 216-230.

CHECKLIST OF THE EXHIBITION

All images are pigment inkjet on paper, printed in 2002. Dimensions are in inches.

PORT REPUBLIC

Moss Mill Road, Port Republic, New Jersey, 1990, 22 x 44

Beers Comstock and Cline Map, Port Republic, New Jersey, 1990, 22 x 44

Alexander Smith Grave, Port Republic, New Jersey, 1990, 22 x 35

Charles Boling Grave, Port Republic, New Jersey, 1990, 22 x 35

Josiah Boling Grave, Port Republic, New Jersey, 1990, 22 x 35

Samuel S. Boling Grave, Port Republic, New Jersey, 1990, 22 x 35

William Lee Grave, Port Republic, New Jersey, 1990, 22 x 35

Boling Children at School, Port Republic, New Jersey, 1911, 22 x 35

MORRIS BEACH

View of Morris Beach from Jobs Point Road, Morris Beach, New Jersey, 2000, 22 x 44

Bethune Avenue, Morris Beach, New Jersey, 2000, 22 x 44

Former Community Center, Morris Beach, New Jersey, 2000, 22 x 44

Jack Trower's House, Morris Beach, New Jersey, 2000, 22 x 44

WHITESBORO

Whitesboro Head Start, Whitesboro, New Jersey, 1990, 22 x 44

Near Route 211, Rosindale, North Carolina, 1991, 22 x 44

Whitesboro New Jersey, 1990, 22 x 44

Audrey Lackey, Real Estate Office, Whitesboro, New Jersey, 1989, 22 x 44

Gladys Spaulding, Whitesboro, New Jersey, 1989, 22 x 44

Paul Reynolds, President Male-Tones Gospel Singers, Whitesboro, New Jersey, 1989, 22 x 44

Woodie Armstrong's Barbershop, Indian Trail Road, Whitesboro, New Jersey, 1989, 22 x 44

Male-Tones Gospel Singers, Whitesboro, New Jersey, 1989, 22 x 44

Alice Jones, Whitesboro, New Jersey, 1989, 22 x 39

Three Girls, Whitesboro, New Jersey, 1989, 22 x 39

Re-Focus on Our Youth!!, Whitesboro, New Jersey, 2001, 22 x 44

Preparing the Grill, Whitesboro, New Jersey, 2001, 22 x 44

Chanice Mathews, Whitesboro, New Jersey, 2002, 22 x 44

FRANKLIN STREET SCHOOL, CAPE MAY

Franklin Street School, Cape May, New Jersey, 2002, 22 x 44

Franklin Street School Classroom, Cape May New Jersey, 2002, 22 x 39

Classroom Window, Franklin Street School, Cape May, New Jersey, 2001, 22 x 30

Franklin Street School, Cape May, New Jersey, 1996, 22 x 39

GOULDTOWN

Trinity A.M.E. Church, Gouldtown, New Jersey, 1993, 22 x 44

SPRINGTOWN

Bethel AME Church, Springtown, New Jersey, 2002, 22 x 44

Laura Aldridge, Bethel AME Church, Springtown, New Jersey, 2002, 22 x 44

Interior, Bethel A.M.E., Springtown, New Jersey, 2002, 22 x 30

United Methodist Church, Springtown, New Jersey, 2000, 22 x 44

Springtown, New Jersey, 1999, 22 x 44

SMALL GLOUCESTER

Mount Zion A.M.E. Church, Small Gloucester, New Jersey, 1998, 22 x 39

Mount Zion A.M.E. Cemetery, Small Gloucester, New Jersey, 1998, 22 x 39

Viola P. Finnaman Grave, Mount Zion A.M.E. Cemetery, Small Gloucester, New Jersey, 2002, 22 x 44

Exterior view of Mount Zion Cemetery, Small Gloucester, New Jersey, 2002, 22 x 30

Re-Dedication Ceremony, Mount Zion A.M.E. Church, Small Gloucester, New Jersey, 2001, 22 x 44

Fredric Minus, Mount Zion A.M.E. Church, Small Gloucester, New Jersey, 2001, 22 x 44

Elaine Edwards and Sarah Lucile Stewart-Mitchell, Small Gloucester, New Jersey, 2001, 22 x 44

Richardson Avenue School, Small Gloucester, New Jersey, 1999, 22 x 39

ELSMERE

Robert Tucker, Elsmere, New Jersey, 2002, 22 x 44

Mount Moriah Primitive Baptist Church, Elsmere, New Jersey, 2002, 22 x 44

LAWNSIDE

Clarence Still, Lawnside, New Jersey, 2001, 22 x 44

Peter Mott House, Lawnside, New Jersey, 2001, 22 x 44

Peter Mott House (Ceremony), Lawnside, New Jersey, 2001, 22 x 44

Dedication of Peter Mott House, Lawnside, New Jersey, 2001, 22 x 44

Mount Peace Cemetery, Lawnside, New Jersey, 2001, 22 x 44

Gloria Miller, Alexis Dabney and Pamela Miller Dabney, Carl Miller Funeral Home, Lawnside, New Jersey, 2002, 22 x 44

Lawnside Roll of Honor, Lawnside, New Jersey, 2002, 22 x 30

CHESILHURST

Chesilhurst Boro Hall, Chesilhurst, New Jersey, 1993, 22 x 39

Mayor Arland Poindexter, Chesilhurst, New Jersey, 1992, 22 x 39

Dr. Merrie Hill, Chesilhurst, New Jersey, 1993, 22 x 39

Grant A.M.E. Church, Chesilhurst, New Jersey, c. 1950, 22 x 39

Grant A.M.E. Church Office, Chesilhurst, New Jersey, 1993, 22 x 39

Cemetery, Chesilhurst, New Jersey, 1993, 22 x 39

First Baptist Church, Chesilhurst, New Jersey, 1993, 22 x 30

Pleasant Harrison, Chesilhurst, New Jersey, 1994, 22 x 39

Reverend James Saylor, Chesilhurst, New Jersey, 1993, 22 x 39

Tecolia Salters, Chesilhurst, New Jersey, 1994, 22 x 39

ADAT BEYT MOSHEH

Adat Beyt Mosheh Congregation, Near Elwood, New Jersey, 2002, 22 x 44

Adat Beyt Mosheh Community, Near Elwood, New Jersey, 2002, 22 x 44

Adat Beyt Mosheh, Near Elwood, New Jersey, 2002, 22 x 44

Respes Family in Adat Beyt Mosheh, Near Elwood, New Jersey, 2002, 22 x 44

NEWTONVILLE

Dugout House, Newtonville, New Jersey, 2001, 22 x 44

Michelle Washington Wilson, Newtonville, New Jersey 2001, 22 x 35

Cemetery, Newtonville, New Jersey, 1995, 22 x 44

Panoramas

Classroom, Franklin Street School, Cape May, New Jersey, 2002, 20 x 144

Cemetery, Small Gloucester, New Jersey, 2002, 20 x 144

Tiffany's Beans, Greens, and Birds, Whitesboro, New Jersey, 2001, 20 x 144

Bethel A.M.E. Church, Springtown, New Jersey, 2002, 20 x 144

Multimedia

Video Projection, *Small Towns, Black Lives* multimedia web presentation, 2002

FURTHER READING

DeCarava, Roy, and Langston Hughes. *Sweet Flypaper of Life.* New York: Hill and Wang 1955. Reprinted Washington, D. C.: Howard University Press, 1984.

Dent, David J. *In Search of Black America: Discovering the African American Dream.* New York: Simon & Schuster, 2000.

Goodman, Mark. *A Kind of History.* San Francisco: Marker Books, 1999.

Green, Shirley, ed. *History of Whitesboro.* Whitesboro, N. J.: Whitesboro History Foundation, 1998.

Lee, Jareena. "Sisters of the Spirit." Bloomington, Indiana University Press, 1986.

Morris, Wright. *The Inhabitants.* 1946. Reprinted, New York, Da Capo Press, 1971.

Morris, Wright. *God's Country and My People.* 1968. Reprinted, Lincoln, Nebr., University of Nebraska Press, 1981.

Peterson, Carla L. *Doers of the Word: African American Women Speakers and Writers in the North (1830 - 1880).* New Brunswick, N.J.: Rutgers University Press, 1995.

Price, Clement Alexander. *Freedom Not Far Distant: A Documentary History of Afro-Americans in New Jersey.* Newark, N.J.: New Jersey Historical Society, 1980.

Price, Clement Alexander, Spencer R. Crew, and Herbert J. Foster. *The Black Experience in Southern New Jersey.* Camden N.J.: Camden County Historical Society, 1985.

Rodriguez, Luis. *The Republic of East L.A.* New York: HarperCollins, 2002.

Sernett, Milton ed. *African American Religious History: A Documentary Witness.* Durham, N.C.: Duke University Press, 1999.

Steward, William, Theophilus G. Steward. *Gouldtown: A Very Remarkable Settlement of Ancient Date.* Philadelphia: J. B. Lippincott, 1913.

Still, James. *Early Recollections and Life of Dr. James Still,* 1877. Reprinted Freeport, New York: Books for Libraries Press, 1971

Trotter, Jr., Joe William and Eric Ledell Smith, eds. *African Americans In Pennsylvania, Shifting Historical Perspectives.* University Park, Pa.: Pennsylvania State University Press, 1997.

Trusty, Emma Marie. *The Underground Railroad: Ties that Bound, Unveiled.* Philadelphia: Amed Literary, 1999.

Turner, William. *America's Black Towns and Settlements.* Rohnert Park, Calif.: Missing Pages Productions, 1998.

Williams, William E. *Gettysburg: A Journey in Time.* Philadelphia: Esther M. Klein Art Gallery, 1997.

Wright, Giles R. *Afro-Americans in New Jersey: a short history.* Trenton: New Jersey Historical Commission, 1989

WENDEL A. WHITE
ARTIST BIOGRAPHY

Wendel A. White was born in Newark, New Jersey 1956 and grew up in New York City, Philadelphia, and New Jersey. He was introduced to photography as a high school student at Montclair High School, Montclair, New Jersey. In 1979 he was awarded a BFA in photography from the School of Visual Arts in New York and in 1982, an MFA in photography from the University of Texas at Austin. In 1982 he moved to Brooklyn and in 1986, to New Jersey, where he currently lives with his wife and daughter.

His work has been included in various museum and corporate collections, individual and group exhibitions, and publications. A complete listing is available on-line at blacktowns.org.

White began teaching photography as a volunteer instructor for the high school art program operated within Bellevue Psychiatric Hospital; later he taught classes at the School of Visual Arts, International Center for Photography, and Cooper Union. In 1986, continuing to exhibit and produce new photographic works based on urban and industrial settings, he accepted a position on the faculty of Richard Stockton College of New Jersey.

In 1993 he was elected to the board of directors for the Society for Photographic Education and served as board chair from 1996 to 1999. White served on the Kodak Educational Advisory Council from 1991 to 1994 and on boards for various cultural organizations in New Jersey, among them, Save Outdoor Sculpture and the Atlantic City Historical Museum.

The *Small Towns, Black Lives* project began in mid-1989 and images from the Port Republic community were exhibited between 1990 and 1995 as part of the traveling exhibition *Convergence: 8 Photographers*. In 1991 he went to the Center for Creative Imaging in Maine and began using the computer in artworks based on an earlier series of manipulated landscapes. This led to the creation of a web-based presentation of the Port Republic images that went on-line in 1993 as a web site called *The Cemetery* (the images are now included as part of *Small Towns, Black Lives*.) The site included the photographs and text from the *Convergence* exhibition plus hypertext links to images of the archival documents that were used to construct the story of the black community that no longer existed.

ACKNOWLEDGEMENTS

The contributions and support of individual residents in the various communities is the very core of what has made this project possible. However, I am especially grateful to Rev. George Thompson, Shirley Green, Laura Aldridge, Freida Bentley, Robert P. Tucker, Clarence Still, Manuel Respes, Michelle Washington Wilson, and Elaine Edwards for sharing their personal experiences and for serving as facilitators and guides to communities and history.

During the past thirteen years my momentum has been sustained and renewed by individuals and institutions closely associated with my profession. The Richard Stockton College of New Jersey faculty, students and administrators have all been part of a process that enabled me to do this work. Fellowships from the Stockton College Distinguished Faculty Fellowship Committee and the Research and Professional Development Committee as well as support from the New Jersey Council for the Arts and the Eastman Kodak Educational Advisory Council have provided support and encouragement. Individual recognition is due to a few friends that have influenced this project directly and indirectly, some through contact as brief as a conversation and others with ongoing input; Jules Allen, Vicki Gold-Levi, Mark Goodman, Lou Draper, Ken Tompkins, William Williams, and Deborah Willis.

The catalogue has become a substantially satisfying portion of the exhibition because of the thoughtful generosity of Deborah Willis, Stedman Graham, and Clement A. Price. Their essays provide a rich experience for the reader and I thank each of them for participating with the museum to create this book. I am deeply grateful for the contributions of Mary Christian as editor, advisor and partner in the process. Carole LoBue of the Stockton College division of Arts and Humanities made sure that Mary's carefully edited pages were accurately transcribed. Karen Quinn's elegant designs for several of the support materials have been a true asset to this project.

The Noyes Museum of Art has been a great partner throughout the project and I am appreciative of all the work by the staff and the commitment of the trustees. This exhibition was originally formulated and conceived by Hsiao-Ning Tu of the Noyes Museum, whose dedication and perseverance gave it life. Charles Stainback, of the Tang Museum, has guided the exhibition and the catalogue with professionalism, intelligence, and thoughtfulness.

The influence of my family within this project is significant. In many ways the images are connected to the stories and remembrances of my childhood. My mother, Symera H. White and her brothers provided me with a background of experience that cannot be separated from these images. My father and stepmother, Howard and Evelyn White, are a continual source of support, faith in my work, and love. The final and most significant recognition and thanks are for the two people that have made great sacrifices for me and the project—my wife, Carmela Colon-White, and daughter, Amanda R. White.